"The life growth stages of a Butterfly"

Hello, my name is Sweetie. I am a butterfly.

And, I would like to tell you, all about the beginning steps of how I grew into a butterfly!

I grew into a butterfly with one step at a time!

A Butterfly has four stages of a life cycle.

The first stage of a butterfly's life begins as a small round egg.

Eggs are laid
out on the
leaves of
plants.

Next stage is the larva which is now a caterpillar.

Caterpillars are
short, stubbby and
have no wings.

The caterpillar is the feeding stage; so, all they do is eat.

The caterpillar will eat the leaf they are born onto first, and is important to the mother butterfly.

Caterpillars like
to eat only
certain leaves.

Caterpillars need to eat often, and a lot so they can grow quickly.

When the caterpillar becomes full grown it stops eating.

The caterpillar will form into the pupa, which is the third stage of growing.

The caterpillar starts forming its' tiny legs and organs inside of the pupa.

Inside of the pupa is where a beautiful butterfly is growing.

In just a few hours a butterfly has grown into adulthood.

The beautiful butterfly can now fly and the life of another butterfly begins.

The adult butterfly than lays eggs on the plant leaf.

Then larva; which becomes the caterpillar!

The caterpillar now grows inside of the pupa.

I am now a full-grown butterfly!

There are live butterfly kits where you may see the entire cycle and birth of a butterfly.

You could watch them eat, crawl and grow into a beautiful butterfly!

It is important, that you let the butterfly, fly back out into the nature of outdoors to live their own life.

The butterfly is important to nature, as they are pollinators to flowers, and the larvae becomes food for other insects.

The End

You may also
Enjoy these
books:
Mr. Woody, Mr.
Sniff; or Chyna
Bug

www.ingramcontent.com/pod-product-compliance
Lightning Source LLC
Chambersburg PA
CBHW060814290526
45792CB00005BA/1647